Desiderata

Desiderata

A Poem for a Way of Life

Max Ehrmann

Illustrations by Sally Sturman

Crown Publishers, Inc.
New York

Published by Crown Publishers, Inc., 201 East 50th Street,
New York, New York 10022.
CROWN is a trademark of Crown Publishers, Inc.

Book design by Linda Kocur
with Nancy Kenmore

Manufactured in the United States of America

Library of Congress Cataloging in Publication Data
Ehrmann, Max, 1872-1945.
Desiderata/by Max Ehrmann—1st ed.
I. Title. II. Title: Poem for a way of life
PS3509.H7D38 1995
818'.5202—dc20   95-30216
                                    CIP
ISBN 0-517-70183-9
10 9 8 7 6 5 4 3 2 1
First Edition

Desiderata

Go placidly amid the noise & haste,

& remember what
peace there may be in silence.

As far as possible without
surrender

*be on good terms with
all persons.*

*Speak your truth quietly &
clearly; and listen to others,*

even to the dull &
the ignorant; they too
have their story.

Avoid loud & aggressive persons,

they are vexatious to the spirit.

If you compare yourself with others, you may become vain or bitter;

for always there will be greater
& lesser persons than yourself.

Enjoy your achievements

as well as your plans.

Keep interested in your own career, however humble;

*it is a real possession in the
changing fortunes of time.*

Exercise caution in your
business affairs;

for the world is full of trickery.

But let not this blind you to what virtue there is; many persons strive for high ideals;

and everywhere life is full
of heroism.

Be yourself.

Especially, do not feign affection.

*Neither be cynical about love; for
in the face of all aridity &
disenchantment*

it is as perennial as the grass.

Take kindly the counsel
of the years,

gracefully surrendering the
things of youth.

Nurture strength of spirit

to shield you
in sudden misfortune.

But do not distress yourself with dark imaginings.

Many fears are born of fatigue & loneliness.

Beyond a wholesome discipline,

be gentle with yourself.

You are a child of the universe,
no less than the trees &
the stars;

you have a right to be here.

And whether or not it is clear to you,

no doubt the universe is unfolding as it should.

Therefore be at peace with God,

whatever you conceive Him to be.

And whatever your labors &
aspirations, in the noisy
confusion of life

keep peace in your soul.

With all its sham, drudgery &
broken dreams,

it is still a beautiful world.

Be cheerful.

Strive to be happy.

Desiderata, which is usually said to have been copied from an inscription "found in Old Saint Paul's Church, Baltimore; dated 1692," was actually written by an Indiana poet named Max Ehrmann and registered with the Copyright Office of the Library of Congress early in 1927. Copyright was renewed after the author's death by his widow, and the work still is protected by the United States Copyright Law. Thus, this popular philosophical statement is neither anonymous nor ancient, having both an author and a fairly recent date. Nonetheless, what it says remains timeless and reserves for its author a niche in that poetical pantheon to which belong those writers who have, at least once, seen an eternal truth clearly.